My WeiRD School
FAST FACTS

Space, Humans, and Farts

Also by Dan Gutman

My WeiRd School
FAST FACTS

Space, Humans, and Farts

Dan Gutman

Pictures by
Jim Paillot

HARPER
An Imprint of HarperCollinsPublishers

To Emma

The author gratefully acknowledges the editorial contributions of Laurie Calkhoven.

Photograph credits: page 11: Education Images / Getty; 16: Jeff Greenberg / Getty; 22: Macrovector / Shutterstock; 25: DEA / D'ARCO EDITORI / Getty; 26: Bettmann / Getty; 34: Encyclopedia Britannica / Getty; 40: Herbert / Getty; 51: Chanwut Jukrachai / Shutterstock; 54: Dimitry Feoktistov / Getty; 57: Vladimir Larionov / Getty; 61: NASA / Getty; 70: Karim Sahib / Getty; 78: S. Kuelcue / Shutterstock; 85: Arterra / Getty; 90: DEA / W. Buss / Getty; 92: Waring Abbott / Getty; 106: Skyhawk x / Shutterstock; 110: Alila Medical Media / Shutterstock; 116: Steve Christo / Getty; 118: Bruce Dale / Getty; 122: Alain Jocard / Getty; 127: Sovfoto / Getty; 130: Hulton Archive / Getty; 134: Bettmann / Getty; 139: Boyer / Getty; 145: Maurice Ambler / Getty; 146: David Goddard / Getty; 172: Richard Heathcote / Getty

ISBN 978-0-06-230626-5 (trade bdg.) — ISBN 978-0-06-230627-2 (lib. bdg.)

22 23 BRR 10 9 8
❖
First Edition

Contents

The Beginning

 My name is Professor A.J. and I know everything there is to know about science.

 You probably don't know *anything* about science, Arlo.

Oh no! It's Andrea Young, that annoying girl in my class with curly brown hair! She calls me by my real name because she knows I don't like it. Well, it just so happens that I know a *lot* about science, because my great-uncle Ernie was a scientist.

 Is that so?

 Yes, that's so. You've heard of the law of gravity. Well, my great-uncle Ernie discovered the law of towels.

 I never heard of a law of towels, Arlo. What is it?

The law of towels states that a towel can never get dirty, because we use it to dry ourselves off when we get out of the shower or wash our hands. We're clean, so the towel has to be clean. That's why towels can never get dirty. It's the law of towels!

 That's just ridiculous, Arlo, and you know it!

 Yeah, some kids will fall for *anything* they read in a book! But I know lots of *real* science facts too. I bet you didn't know that the average person produces about three pounds of earwax in their lifetime. That's a true science fast fact!

Look it up if you don't believe me.

 Nobody cares about the science of earwax, Arlo. We're here to talk about *important* science stuff.

 Says who? Earwax is important! I know all about the science of earwax, farts, boogers, poop, and snot too. I could write a whole book about it. Hey, we should do the whole book about the science of grossness!

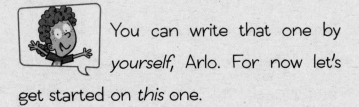 You can write that one by *yourself*, Arlo. For now let's get started on *this* one.

Okay, okay. But I want to tell the readers one last thing before we get started. On the last page of this book, I'm going to reveal the secret of the universe. So if you just can't wait to learn the secret, turn to the last page of this book right now.*

Sincerely,

Professor A.J.

(the professor of awesomeness)

 Andrea Young, PhD

(This is going to help me get into Harvard someday.)

---

* I'm not kidding. Do it!

Chapter 1

The Why Game

Hi everybody! My name is Mr. Docker, and I'm the science teacher at Ella Mentry School. Andrea and A.J. asked me to help them tell you a little about science. I'm happy to help. I guess I should start from the beginning. Science is knowledge of the world learned through experiments and observation.

Okay, that makes no sense at all, Mr. Docker.

 Perhaps I can explain in simpler terms, A.J. Science is how we learn new things. It's all about asking questions and trying to find answers to them.

Do you mean questions like: Why do scientists seem so nerdy? Why is science so boring? How do I get an A in science class?

 No, Arlo! Mr. Docker means asking questions that will help us learn about the world around us.

Questions like: Why is the sky blue? Why do elephants have long trunks? Am I right, Mr. Docker?

 That's right, Andrea! I think kids make great scientists because you're naturally curious.

I have a good science question. When snow melts and turns into water, where does the white go?

Huh? What? Hmm, I never really thought about that, A.J. But the point I'm trying to make is that anyone can be a scientist. All you have to do is look around and ask "Why?" I love it

when kids ask Why questions.

 I have a good Why question. Is it true that sound can't travel through a vacuum?

 Yes, that's true, A.J. That's a fact.

 Well, if sound can't travel through a vacuum, why are vacuum cleaners so loud?

 Wait. What? Is that a joke?

 If ice floats, why is Antarctica

at the bottom of the world? Shouldn't it be at the top?

 Uh, hmmm, I don't know. Will you look at the time! It's getting late. I need to go.

 Why do meteors always land in craters?

 Umm, I never thought about that. . . .

Gosses Bluff meteor crater

Why does toast always land butter side down?

 I . . . have to go to a meeting right now, but I'll check back with you two in a little while to see how you're making out.

 Ugh, gross! We're not going to make out!

• • • • • • • • • • • • • •

TRY THIS! Play the Why Game. Here's how you play: Ask your mom or dad a question. Any question. No matter what they answer, ask "Why?" And then when they answer *that*, ask "Why?" again. Then just keep asking "Why?" no matter what they say. At first they're going to be happy that you seem so curious about the world. But very soon they'll realize that you're just being annoying. See how many times you can ask "Why?" before your parents tell you to knock it off. My record is nine.

Chapter 2

Mr. Docker Explains the Scientific Method

 Before A.J. and Andrea give you all their fast facts, I should explain the scientific method. This is the process scientists use to learn things. You can use it too.

The scientific method always begins with

a question. The question would be about something you want to know. Let's say your question is, What color are pumpkins?

Next you (the scientist) will do some research on the subject. You might read articles about pumpkins. You might go online and search for websites about pumpkins. You might see what other scientists have discovered about pumpkins.

Now it's time for you to come up with your hypothesis. That's a fancy word that basically means a guess. Let's say your hypothesis is: Pumpkins are blue.

Next you need to run an experiment to see if your hypothesis is true. You might gather a hundred people in a room, show them a bunch of pumpkins, and ask them to write on a piece of paper what color the pumpkins are.

Then the results need to be collected, recorded, and tallied up. Let's say ninety-nine

of the hundred people wrote "ORANGE," and one smart aleck wrote "My cousin's pumpkin wrote the Declaration of Independence." You can look at the results and be reasonably sure that your hypothesis was wrong. Pumpkins are *not* blue. You also wasted a lot of time on a silly experiment.

But just to be sure, you need to do the experiment all over again to make sure the results weren't just an accident or a coincidence.

Finally, your last step as a scientist is to come to a conclusion and share the results with the world. You would publish it in a scientific journal that will be read by other scientists. Because your results didn't prove your hypothesis, you might start all over again with a *new* hypothesis: Pumpkins are red!

That example was kind of silly, but that's how the scientific method works. All scientists use it.

Before we had the scientific method to learn about the world, silly rumors and superstitions would be accepted as facts. During the Middle Ages, some doctors believed that diseases were caused by having too much blood in the body. So they would do a "bloodletting." Yes, to heal people, they would cut open that person so he or she would bleed. You can imagine how *that* worked out.

Just a few hundred years ago, tomatoes

were considered to be poisonous. That's right! No pizza. No spaghetti with meat sauce. What happened was that in parts of Europe during the late 1700s, many people died after eating tomatoes. The tomato was called the "poison apple."

But it wasn't the tomatoes that killed people. It was because wealthy people ate off pewter plates, which were made from lead. Tomatoes are very acidic, so the lead leached off the plates into the tomatoes, and people got lead poisoning. If they had used the scientific method back then and done a simple experiment using different kinds of plates, they would have learned it was the *plates* that were poisonous, not the tomatoes.

It's good that we have science and the scientific method. Science has made our lives easier. Science has taught us a lot about our planet. Science has even allowed us to leave our planet and explore outer space. Speaking of which . . .

Chapter 3

Far-Out: Our Solar System

 A solar system is made up of a star (like our sun) and all the planets and other bodies that orbit around it. I'll let A.J. and Andrea give you some fast facts about the solar system. . . .

 Did you know that we live inside the sun? It's true! The sun itself is a huge, hot ball of light ninety-three million miles away. But actually, the sun's outer atmosphere extends far beyond its surface. The earth orbits around the sun inside this outer atmosphere.

If the earth was much closer to the sun, it would be too hot to support life. If it was much farther away, it would be too *cold* to support life. So it's lucky that we're right in the middle of hot and cold.

Remember the story of Goldilocks and the three bears? Goldilocks tastes the first bowl of porridge and says it's too hot. She finds the next bowl and says it's too cold. But she finds the third one and says it's "just right." That's why scientists say we live in the "Goldilocks Zone."

 Every time the earth spins around, it's one day (that's

twenty-four hours). And every time it makes an orbit around the sun, it's one year (365 days). But actually, it takes 365 *plus a quarter of a day* to go around the sun. To correct for that, every four years, at the end of February, we add one "leap day" to the year. So if your birthday is February 29, you only get a birthday every four years. Nah-nah-nah boo-boo on you!

 The earth is not straight up and down. It's tilted a little. That's why we have seasons. As the earth moves around the sun during the year, some parts get more direct sunlight than other parts. When the northern parts of the planet (like North America, where our school is) are titled toward the sun, it's summer here. When we're tilted away from the sun, it's winter.

The longest day of the year (at least in the Northern Hemisphere) always falls between June 20 and 22. That's the "summer solstice," and it's the first day of summer. The shortest day of the year is between December 20 and 23. That's called the "winter solstice," and it's the first day of winter.

Comets, asteroids, meteoroids, meteors, and meteorites are part of the solar system too. What's the difference between all those things? I thought you'd never ask.

A comet is an object in outer space that orbits the sun and is made of ice, dust, and rocks. It has a long, bright tail.

Halley's Comet, 1986

An asteroid is a lot like a comet, but it's made mostly out of metal and doesn't have a tail.

26

A meteoroid is a small body that moves in the solar system.

If it enters the earth's atmosphere, it's called a meteor.

If it hits the ground, it's called a meteorite.

And if it hits your house, I hope you won't be home.

 The other planets that make up our solar system are interesting too. Here are a few fast facts about each one. . . .

Mercury: Even though it's the closest planet to the sun, scientists think there might be ice inside the craters on its north and south poles.

Venus: It rotates in the opposite direction of all the other planets. It also spins very *slowly*. So a day on Venus is longer than a year on Venus. That must be weird.

 Mars: Olympus Mons on Mars is the biggest volcano in the solar system—it's three times as tall as Mount Everest!

Mt. Everest   OLYMPUS MONS

 Jupiter: It has wild winds that blow its thick red, orange,

brown, and white clouds around. The winds also move Jupiter's Great Red Spot—a huge storm that's lasted for 350 years! The storm is more than three times the size of Earth.

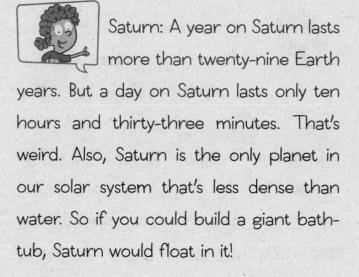

Saturn: A year on Saturn lasts more than twenty-nine Earth years. But a day on Saturn lasts only ten hours and thirty-three minutes. That's weird. Also, Saturn is the only planet in our solar system that's less dense than water. So if you could build a giant bathtub, Saturn would float in it!

Neptune: If you like sailing or windsurfing, you should

go to Neptune. It has the strongest winds in the solar system. They move as fast as fifteen *hundred* miles per hour! On second thought, maybe you shouldn't go there.

 Uranus: All the other planets spin around like tops. But Uranus spins the *other* way, like a ball rolling down a hill. So the north pole or south pole is usually pointed toward the sun. If you could stand on the north pole of Uranus, you would see the sun rise in the sky and circle around for forty-two *years*. Then it would dip down below the horizon, and you would be sitting in the dark for forty-two years.

Plus, it's called Uranus.

 Pluto: It used to be a planet. Then it got demoted to a "dwarf planet."

 Oh, snap! In Pluto's face! When someone or something gets demoted, we say it got "plutoed."

 Okay, let's go back down to Earth now and talk about the nitty-gritty of science.*

---

* Hi! Having a nice day? Good. Okay, you can go back to reading the book now.

Does Matter Matter?

Everything in the world is made of something we scientists call "matter."

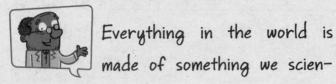

Okay, that makes no sense at all. Does matter matter?

Yes! Matter is an object that

has mass and occupies space. Many scientists believe there's a limited amount of matter in the universe.

 Wait, I don't get it. If there's only a limited amount of matter in the universe, how do you explain those all-you-can-eat buffets?

 Wait. What?

 Very funny, Arlo! Let Mr. Docker explain.

 Let me put it this way. An atom is the smallest particle of a substance that exists. Atoms are *really* tiny. In fact, a million atoms would fit on the head of a pin.

 WOW! That's "MOM" upside down, by the way.

 And atoms are made up of even smaller particles called protons, electrons, and neutrons.

When two or more atoms join together, they're called a molecule. Let's look at the

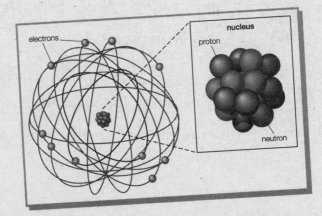

most common type of molecule that you kids might be familiar with.

 A pizza molecule?

 Actually, I was thinking of a *water* molecule.

 My mom told me that water is also called H_2O.

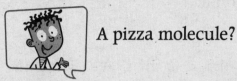 Yes, H_2O is the chemical symbol for water. One molecule of water is made from two atoms of hydrogen and one atom of oxygen.

Water is cool because you can drink it, and you can also go ice-skating on it.

 Not only that, A.J., but water also makes clouds in the sky.

 Huh? What?

 You see, matter can take three forms: solid, liquid, or gas. And water is the only substance on Earth that naturally exists in all three states. First, of course, it's a liquid, which we can drink, wash ourselves with, swim in, water the lawn with, and things like that.

 In most cases, if it's 32 degrees Fahrenheit, water turns into a solid: ice. You can put ice in a drink to cool it or put it on a sprained ankle to reduce the swelling.

 Or go ice-skating on it.

Right. And if you put a pot of it on the stove and heat it to 212°F, it boils and turns into a gas: water vapor. On hot, humid days, you can feel the water vapor in the air. When it rises higher and cools off, it will become a cloud. Clouds are just billions of water droplets that join together and float in the air. But mostly you can't see water vapor. It's invisible. Can you kids come up with any other fast facts about water?

 Yes! We can live without food for about two months. But we can only live about a week without water.

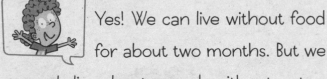 About 70 percent of our planet is covered with water.

Almost all that water is salt water in the oceans. We can't drink it. Only about 3 percent is freshwater: drinkable water. And most of that drinkable water is frozen in the Arctic and in Antarctica. So only about *1 percent* of the world's water is available as drinking water.

 All the water that exists on Earth has been here for billions of years, and we're not getting any more. So don't waste it! Turn off the faucet when you're brushing your teeth. Stop leaks. Take shorter showers. Tell Mom and Dad to fill the dishwasher before running it.

Very good! Snow is made of water too, you know. Snow falls when water vapor attaches to dust particles in the air and freezes. If you look at a snowflake under a microscope, it's a six-sided crystal. And every single one of them is different.

I have one more question about water. If a water molecule is made from two atoms of hydrogen and one atom of oxygen, does that mean I'm drinking hydrogen every time I take a gulp of water?

Yes! Hydrogen occurs naturally as a gas, and it is the lightest thing in the world. Years ago, they used to fill blimps with hydrogen to keep them up in the air. The problem is that hydrogen burns very easily. After a famous blimp called the *Hindenburg* exploded in 1937, they stopped using hydrogen for that purpose.

But the nice thing about hydrogen is that it makes no pollution when it burns.

Someday we may have cars that run on hydrogen.

 So what keeps blimps up in the air today?

 I know! Helium. Like the stuff they put in balloons. It's the *second* lightest gas. It keeps balloons aloft because it's lighter than air.

 How did you know that, Arlo?

 I read it in a book about helium. It was such a good book that I couldn't put it down.

Very funny, Arlo. I have a question. Why does helium make your voice sound funny when you inhale it?

 You kids have a lot of questions! I like that! Because helium is so light, if you breathe it in, the sound waves in your vocal tract travel through it faster—more than twice as fast. So you are changing the gas molecules in your vocal tract and increasing the speed of the sound of your voice. Breathing in helium can be funny at a party, but be careful, because if you breathe in too much of it, it can be dangerous. It's much smarter to breathe air.

Andrea is filled with hot air. I'm surprised that she doesn't rise up off the ground.

 I'm just going to ignore that, Arlo.

 Oxygen is probably the most important thing on Earth. If you don't breathe it, you die. All living things use it. In the water, fish absorb it using their gills. But air isn't made of *just* oxygen. It's made of oxygen, nitrogen, and also small amounts of thirteen other gases, like krypton.

 Krypton? That's where Superman came from! Hey, learning about atoms and stuff is cool.

 Atoms are a lot like you, Arlo.

 Why?

 Because they can't sit still.

 Oh, snap! In my face!

 That's true, Andrea. Atoms are always moving around. The

faster an object's atoms move, the more heat it has. If we could get atoms to stop moving, the object would be completely cold. That temperature would be "absolute zero"— minus 459.67°F.

• • • • • • • • • • • • • • •

TRY THIS! Take a can of soda outside. Shake it up good. Be careful. Pull the tab. What happens?

Gases can expand and contract. When you pump air into your bike tire, you're squeezing that air into a smaller space. Carbon dioxide gas has been squeezed inside your soda can under pressure. When you shake the can and open it, the gas bubbles expand quickly and shoot the soda out the opening.

Try *this* too! Drop a Mentos candy into a bottle of Diet Coke. The candy looks smooth, but there are lots of tiny holes in it. Bubbles form around it. They want to get out. The Mentos is heavy, so it sinks to the bottom of the bottle. The bubbles turn to foam. The pressure builds. And then, *BAM!* Scientists call this "nucleation."

I call it fun.

Chapter 5

Materials—Stuff about Stuff

 Materials are things we can use to make other things.

 Okay, that makes no sense at all. Do you mean *stuff*?

 Uh, yes. Stuff. We scientists usually call it "*material.*"

We know lots of stuff about stuff! Here are some fast facts. . . .

 Do you know what glass is made out of? Sand! It's true. That's why it makes sense that glass was first made in sandy places like Syria, Mesopotamia, and Egypt. Archaeologists have found pieces of glass that date back to 3500 BCE.

Of all the stuff we have, glass is some of the most useful. It's really easy to shape it, clean it, color it, and see through it. It lasts a long time. It resists water, heat, cold, and decay; and it can be recycled easily.

Of course, it can break easily too. But can you imagine a world without windows? A world without mirrors? How would we know what we look like? If I didn't have a mirror, I wouldn't be able to fix my hair.

 Your hair is broken?

Very funny, Arlo. And now they have "safety glass." It uses a thin layer of resin between two layers of glass so it doesn't fly around and hurt people when it breaks. That is perfect for the windshield of a car.

Silk comes from worms. So if you wear a silk blouse, you're wearing something that used to be inside a worm! Gross! A silkworm will spend weeks eating mulberry leaves and lettuce. It will eat fifty *thousand* times its own weight of that stuff. Then it uses its salivary glands to produce this gooey stuff called "fibroin." With that, it starts spinning a cocoon. A silkworm spends the next forty-eight hours turning around and around to create silk.

Silkworms feed on mulberry leaves.

Cotton comes from a plant. So the T-shirt you're wearing right now grew out of the *ground*. It was about seven thousand years ago that somebody in what is now Pakistan figured out that the cotton plant could be a food *and* a fabric. That's right. Cottonseed is used as feed for cattle and can also be made into oil and margarine.

Cotton can absorb up to twenty-seven times its own weight in water.

Thomas Edison's first successful lightbulb used a filament that was made from cotton.

A baseball has 150 yards of cotton inside it.

 One bale of cotton can be made into 215 pairs of jeans or 313,600 hundred-dollar bills.* So paper money is *not* made out of paper!

 Wool comes from sheep. Their fleece is just sheared off, like the sheep are getting a haircut. It doesn't hurt.

---

* I'll take the bills!

The record time for shearing a sheep is 37.9 seconds.

 People have been making wool into clothing since the Bronze Age.

 Wool can be used to make lanolin, which can be used in lip balm, moisturizer, and shoe polish.

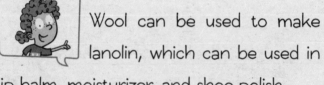 Sheep wool is even used for the insulation in houses!

For centuries, all clothing was made from natural stuff like silk, cotton, and wool. Then in 1935, an American chemist named Wallace Hume mixed some chemicals together (like hexamethylenediamine, if you must know) and created a *synthetic* fiber that came to be called "nylon."

Synthetic fiber is strong, warm, light, water resistant, smooth, stretchy, and cheap. Today, almost half the clothing in the world is made from synthetic fiber. Synthetic fiber is also used in everything from backpacks to parachutes.

Do you know what the hardest stuff in the world is?

Diamonds?

Wrong! So nah-nah-nah boo-boo on you! Diamonds *used to be* the hardest stuff in the world. But then some scientists at North Carolina State University created some new stuff called Q-carbon by shooting laser beams at carbon. They hope to someday use it to make synthetic body parts, deep-water drills, and screens for televisions and cell phones.

The nice thing about stuff is that you can make a lot of stuff into new stuff without having to throw away any old stuff. You just use it again. Recycled paper can be made into toilet paper and paper towels. Recycled plastic can be made into a chair, a road, or just about *anything*.

An elephant statue in Russia made from plastic bottles

Aluminum cans and glass bottles can be made into more cans and bottles. Did you know that if we recycled all the aluminum we have today, we would never have to make any more aluminum?

TRY THIS! You can become a one-person recycling center. Instead of throwing stuff away, sell it, swap it with a friend, donate it to a yard sale or thrift store. If we recycle our stuff, we conserve the earth's natural resources, we save money, we use less energy, and we reduce waste and pollution.

 We could talk a lot more about stuff, but we have a lot more stuff to talk about. So we're going to stop talking about stuff now so we can talk about other stuff.

 Like the science of machines, and light, and sound, and famous scientists, and . . .

 And the science of farting, and burping, and pooping, and peeing!

 Arlo! We're not going to talk about those things. This is an important science book.

 That's what *you* think.

Chapter 6

Forces and Machines

 A force is something that pushes or pulls on objects.

 Okay, that makes no sense at all.

 Maybe I can explain, Arlo. Gravity is a force that makes

things fall toward the earth. It *pulls* us down. If it wasn't for gravity, we'd all be floating around in space.

 That would be cool. It would be like when astronauts float around inside the space station.

 Yes! They're weightless. But they haven't *completely* escaped the earth's gravity, because it's gravity that holds the space station in orbit.

Astronaut Joseph Tanner on a spacewalk, September 2006

If we were on the moon right now, we would be able to jump a lot higher and farther. The force of gravity is weaker there because the moon is smaller and lighter than the earth.

 But it's still pretty strong. It's so strong that the moon controls the tides in our oceans. How does that work, Mr. Docker?

 The moon's gravity pulls on the water in the ocean. Let's say the moon is overhead. That's when the water rises up like it's trying to go to the moon. It's high tide. When the moon is on the *other* side of the earth, the ocean slinks back. It's low tide. About every twelve hours, the water level in the ocean rises and falls.

 Do small objects have gravity too?

 Sure! If you drop a book on the floor, the earth is pulling on the book. But the book is also pulling on the earth to meet it, just a little bit.

 So I guess a little magnet has enough force to overcome all the earth's gravity, right? If it didn't, how would it stick to a refrigerator?

 That's right, A.J.! And gravity

is just *one* force. We can use other forces to do things we can't do on our own, sometimes with the help of machines. Anything that lets us take small forces and turn them into big forces is a machine. Gears, wheels, pulleys, and screws are all simple machines. We don't need fuel to run them. Do you know what a lever is?

 Sure. That's when you go to school in the morning and you say good-bye to your mom. You leave her.

No, dumbhead!* A lever is a kind of machine. A seesaw is a lever, right, Mr. Docker?

---

* Why can't an elephant fall on Andrea's head?

Right. Let's say your dad weighs two hundred pounds. He's too heavy for you to pick him up. But if you sit at one end of a seesaw and your dad sits at the other end, it would be possible to pick him up if you place the balancing point far enough away from you.

So if you had a lever big enough, you could pick up the earth! But that would be weird.

Let's look at another force. Do you kids know what friction is?

 Sure. It's the opposite of non-friction. It's a made-up story. Mrs. Roopy taught us that in the library.

 No, dumbhead! Friction is a force that happens when two objects move against each other. It's the force that makes the motion harder.

 That's right, Andrea. Rub your hands together for a few seconds. They feel warm, right? That's because of friction. The rougher the surface, the more friction, and the more friction, the more heat.

Sandpaper has a *lot* of friction. Ice has very little. So we can slip on it. If there isn't any friction, the two things slide easily.

I'll bet you don't know *this* fast fact. When you go ice-skating, the ice melts a tiny bit as you slide over it. Look it up if you don't believe me.

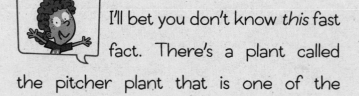I'll bet you don't know *this* fast fact. There's a plant called the pitcher plant that is one of the

slipperiest things in the world. When an insect climbs inside a pitcher plant, the side is so slippery that the insect can't get out. Then it gets eaten by the plant! A plant that eats animals! That's a switch!

 If you ask me, that should be called a catcher plant instead of a pitcher plant.

 Speaking of forces, did you kids ever wonder how a plane can get off the ground? Some of them weigh *hundreds* of tons.

It must be magic.

 It's not magic, Arlo! As the plane rushes down the runway really fast, air rushes over the wings. The wings are curved, making the air faster and the pressure lower above the wing than below it. And that creates an upward force called "lift."

I knew that. And here's a fast fact I bet *you* don't know. Racing cars work the same way, but upside down. They're designed so that the air rushing by pushes them against the road so they can go fast around turns.

Some racing cars can go so fast that they would be able to drive upside down on the ceiling!

• • • • • • • • • • • • • • • • • •

TRY THIS! You can demonstrate lift by sticking your hand out of your car window while your mom or dad is driving down the highway (only do this if there are no cars passing by). Change the angle of your hand and feel it get pushed up or down.

• • • •

 Wait a minute. Helicopters don't rush down a runway.

How do *they* get off the ground?

 Helicopters create lift the same way, but instead of having fixed wings like a plane, they have rotors that spin around. The rotors are like spinning wings.

 Oh, yeah? Then what about rockets? They don't rush down a runway, and they don't have wings or rotors either.

 Rockets use a high-speed blast of burning fuel to create hot gases under pressure. The gases fire backward from the engines to push the rocket upward and into outer space.

It's sort of like when you let the air out of a balloon and the balloon shoots in the opposite direction, right?

Exactly. Rockets and many other machines create the energy they need by burning fossil fuels: oil, coal, and natural gas That's how we can drive cars, heat our houses, turn on electrical appliances, cook food, charge our phones, and so on. The problem is that burning fossil fuel gives off greenhouse gases, and that heats up the atmosphere.

I always hear about the

atmosphere, but I never really knew what it meant.

The atmosphere is the layer of air that surrounds the earth. It extends three hundred miles into space, but most of it is only ten miles deep. That's pretty thin! So if we heat up our atmosphere by continuing to burn fossil fuels, then the ice caps melt, oceans rise, species die out, and soon we will be in real trouble.

 So what can we do about it?

 Gradually, the nations of the world are coming together to make the switch to sources of energy that *don't* involve burning. Solar energy. Wind. Nuclear energy. We can also create energy by harnessing the power of the tides. We can tap into the heat of the earth's core to generate geothermal energy. We can use hydrogen. We need a *lot* of energy, and there are a lot of ways to get it other than by burning things.

That reminds me . . .

Light

Light is a form of energy that radiates through space.

Okay, that makes no sense at all. Everybody knows what light is. It's the reason why we can see stuff! Andrea and I know some cool fast facts about light. . . .

Light travels *really* fast—186,282 miles a second. That means it could travel more than seven times around the earth in one *second*!

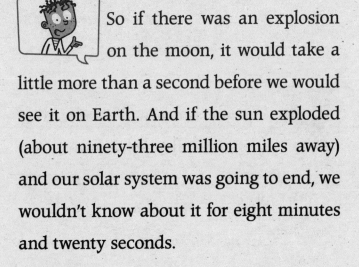 So if there was an explosion on the moon, it would take a little more than a second before we would see it on Earth. And if the sun exploded (about ninety-three million miles away) and our solar system was going to end, we wouldn't know about it for eight minutes and twenty seconds.

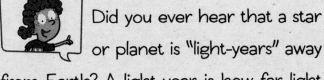 Did you ever hear that a star or planet is "light-years" away from Earth? A light-year is how far light

travels in one year. It's almost six *trillion* miles.

You've probably noticed that during a thunderstorm you see a flash of lightning and then you hear thunder a few seconds later. That's because light travels much faster than sound—almost a million times faster! The thunder and lightning actually happen at the same time. The lightning just reaches your eyes faster.

I know that thunder is a result of the air expanding really fast and vibrating after a lightning bolt. But what *is* lightning, anyway?

Lightning is the discharge of static electricity that builds up in a cloud under certain weather conditions. The air around a flash of lightning is hotter than the surface of the sun.

 I know a cool fast fact about lightning. A single bolt of lightning has enough energy to cook a hundred thousand pieces of toast! I would have liked to see them do *that*

experiment. They must have needed a lot of butter.

 Is lightning like a laser beam?

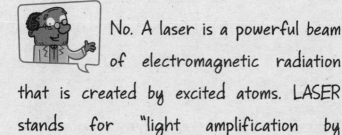 No. A laser is a powerful beam of electromagnetic radiation that is created by excited atoms. LASER stands for "light amplification by

stimulated emission of radiation." A laser is just one color. Instead of spreading out, like sunlight or the beam of a flashlight, all the rays of light go in one direction, so they're very concentrated. That focused beam contains a lot of energy, so we can use it to cut through metal, scan a bar code, perform surgery, and do lots of other things.

 When you play a DVD or a CD, you're using a laser. The laser bounces off the surface of the disc to read the tiny bumps and pits in the disc.

A lens is a curved glass that

bends the light coming into it. There are lenses in your eyes, cameras, eyeglasses, and other things. Different kinds of lenses allow us to see far (telescopes, binoculars) or to see small objects (microscopes, magnifying glasses).

• • • • • • • • • • • • • • •

TRY THIS! Put a pencil in a glass of water. See how the pencil appears to be broken in two at the waterline? That's because the light rays reflecting off the bottom of the pencil have to travel through the water, which slows them down before they reach your eyes. So the pencil looks broken where the air and water meet.

• • • •

Arlo, have you ever seen a movie?

 Sure, I've seen lots of movies.

 No you haven't. There's no such thing as a *moving* picture. Movies are just lots of still pictures that flash by your eyes so quickly that your brain is tricked into thinking the image is moving. Cartoons are lots of drawings that are flashed in front of you the same way.

 Not all living things see light the same way we see it. Cats can see at night much better than people can. It's partly because they have reflecting surfaces in their eyes. Light comes in and then bounces back out, so it passes through their eyes twice. A lot of people think dogs are color-blind. Not true! Dogs can see colors, but they don't see all the colors we do. Mostly, their vision is limited to yellows, blue-violets, and blends of these colors. On the other hand, bees can see colors that we can't.

 Plants can't see, of course. They don't have eyes!* But they take in sunlight and turn it into a sugar called glucose. It's basically plant

---

* What about black-eyed Susans?

food, and it gives the plant energy to grow.

 Speaking of plants, in 2016 a man in Massachusetts grew a pumpkin that weighed over two thousand pounds!

 What does that have to do with light, Arlo?

 Well, the pumpkin wasn't light at all. It was really heavy. So it was the opposite of light.

 You've probably heard the expression "blind as a bat." In

fact, bats are *not* blind. They do have eyes, and they see very well during the day. But at night they fly out and go hunting for food by bouncing sound waves off objects in front of them and listening to the echo of the sound coming back. It's called "echolocation."

So bats can "see" by using sound. Speaking of which . . .

Sound

 Sound is a form of energy that is produced by vibrations.

 Okay, that makes no sense at all.

 Let's say somebody plucks a guitar string. The string vibrates—it moves back and forth. That vibrates the air around the string. That creates sound waves. It's like when you toss a rock in the water and it makes ripples in all directions. You hear vibrations when you hear music, speech, birds chirping, or an explosion.

 When the sound waves reach your ears, they vibrate your eardrums.

 There are drums in my ears? Help! Call 911! I need an ambulance!

 Relax, Arlo! They're just tiny little drums, about ten millimeters wide.

Your eardrums pass along these vibrations to three tiny bones in your middle ears. They are called the hammer, anvil, and stirrup. They're the smallest bones in our bodies. All together, they're smaller than the size of a pea. These bones activate the cochlea, which turn the motion into electrical signals that go to the nerves that communicate with your brain. And *that's* how you hear sound.

When you knock on a door, you make it vibrate so people on the other side can hear it. The faster the vibration, the higher the pitch of the notes.

TRY THIS! Put ten bottles in a line and fill each one with a different amount of water. Now blow air across the top of each bottle. What happens? The air inside the bottles vibrates to make a sound. The more air that's in the bottle, the lower the pitch.

• • • •

Sound waves bounce off objects. When they come back, you may hear an echo. The reason why amphitheaters are curved is not just so many people can see the stage. It also helps the sound echo all "around."

Roman amphitheater at Kom el-Dik

 Sound can be loud or soft, of course. A crying baby can be louder than a car horn. On the other hand, there's a tribe of people in Sudan, Africa, called Maabans who are extremely quiet. Their environment is so quiet, in fact, that they can hear a whisper from across the distance of a baseball field. Scientists studied the tribe and discovered that hearing loss is *not* a result of getting older. We lose our hearing because of all the loud noises we're exposed to every day.

 Just like different animals see light differently, different animals hear sound differently. Dogs, wolves, cats, dolphins, mice, some frogs, and moths have better hearing than we do. Flies, on the other hand, are deaf. They don't have ears. But they can feel vibrations.

Blue whale sculpture at the American Museum of Natural History

 The blue whale is one of the loudest animals in the world. It makes a noise that can be heard five *hundred* miles away.

 Cows make more milk when they listen to music.

 The speed of sound is 768 miles per hour. But sound

travels four times faster than that through water, ten times faster through granite, and *fifteen* times faster through steel.

When a plane travels faster than the speed of sound, it overtakes the sound waves in front of it. It creates what is called a "sonic boom." *Boom!*

Did you ever hear a whip crack? That's a sonic boom. The motion of the whip accelerates so fast that it's going faster than the speed of sound.

• • • • • • • • • • • • • • •

TRY THIS! In the last chapter we said that you see lightning before you hear thunder because the speed of light is faster than the speed of sound. If you want to figure out how far away a thunderstorm is, wait until you see lightning. Then start counting "One Mississippi, two Mississippi," like that. When you hear thunder, stop counting. Divide that number by five. That's how many miles away the storm is.

● ● ● ●

There was a science fiction movie called *Alien* that used the tagline "In space, no one can hear you scream." No one can hear you speak or clap your hands either. There's no sound in space. To be heard, sound needs air, water, or some medium for the sound to travel through.

 So I guess no one can hear you fart or burp in space either.

 We weren't going to talk about that stuff, Arlo. Remember?

 Oh, yeah. I forgot.

"Remember to look up at the stars and not down at your feet."
—Stephen Hawking

It's Alive!

What do you think it means to be alive?

If you poke something with a stick and it doesn't move, it's probably not alive.

Well, a scientist might look at

it differently, A.J. For starters, he or she might say a living thing is made out of cells, it uses energy, it grows, it reproduces, and it responds to its environment.

 Okay, that makes no sense at all. I still say you should poke it with a stick.

 Maybe it would be easier to understand if we started with people, because that's what we are.

 Excellent idea, Andrea! Our species is called *Homo sapiens,* and we first appeared in what is Africa today about two hundred thousand years ago. The human body is fascinating. I just went on the internet and read that the average body has enough iron in it to make a three-inch nail, enough sulfur to kill all the fleas on a dog, enough carbon to make nine hundred pencils, enough fat to make seven bars of soap, and enough water to fill a ten-gallon tank. Can you kids come up with some fast facts about the human body?

 Sure!

Head

 The average brain weighs around three pounds. Andrea's

98

head is a lot lighter than average, of course, because she doesn't have a brain.

 Very funny, Arlo. The left side of your body is controlled by the right side of your brain, and the right side of your body is controlled by the left side of your brain. That's why left-handed people say they're the only ones in their right mind.

 We are all boneheads. That's because there are 22 bones in our head. Speaking of bones, they are the one thing kids have more of than grown-ups. Adults have 206. But we have 300. So we win!

I know what you're thinking. People must lose bones as they grow up. That's weird! Where do the bones go? Well, they don't go anywhere. As we get older, some of our bones fuse together. That's why grown-ups have fewer of them.

And in case you were wondering, bones are *not* pure white. We think they're white because the skeletons in museums have been boiled and cleaned. Human bones are pinkish-white inside your body because of the blood flowing through your bone marrow.

Eyes

 When you were born, your eyes were slightly lighter in color than they are now. That's because the pigmentation of your irises develops in the first year of your life.

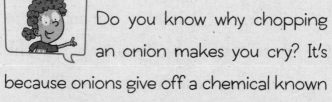 Do you know why chopping an onion makes you cry? It's because onions give off a chemical known as syn-propanethial-S-oxide. It stimulates your lachrymal glands to release tears.

Nose

 My dad has hairs sticking out of his nose, and every few weeks he has to use a little machine to trim them. Gross! He told me that *everybody* has little hairs in their nose, so there must be a reason. Sometimes there's a lot of pollen or cat dander in the air. Maybe there's something you're allergic to. The hairs in your nose trap that stuff. Your body wants to get rid of it, so it makes you sneeze to shoot it out.

 When you sneeze, your mucus will move more than a hundred miles an hour. So cover your mouth,

Arlo, because I don't want that yucky stuff flying all over me.

 It's really hard to sneeze and keep your eyes open at the same time. Just try. That's because your nose and eyes are linked by cranial nerves.

And by the way, iguanas sneeze more than any other animal.

Do you know why pepper makes you

sneeze? It contains some stuff called piperine, which irritates the nerve endings inside your mucous membrane. Your nose wants to kick out this stuff, so it tells your brain, "Sneeze!"

• • • • • • • • • • • • •

TRY THIS! If you sprinkle a bunch of black pepper in a bowl of water, put a dab of soap on the tip of your finger and dip it in the water. All the pepper will go to the opposite side of the bowl.

• • • •

When we eat something we like, we say it tastes good. But flavor is a combination of taste and smell, and it's mostly smell. The next time you eat something, hold your nose closed. You'll probably notice that the food doesn't taste as flavorful.

Lungs

 We have two of them, and you probably think they're exactly the same. They're *not*. Your left lung is divided into two lobes, while your right lung is divided into three. Your left lung is a little bit smaller, which allows room for your heart.

Heart

 Your heart beats around a hundred thousand times a

day. So when you get to be thirty years old, your heart will have beat over a *billion* times. And by the way, women's hearts beat faster than men's hearts. So we win!

Hands and Feet

 Your fingernails grow almost four times faster than your toenails!

 One-fourth of all the bones in your body are in your feet. You'll probably walk 115,000 miles in your

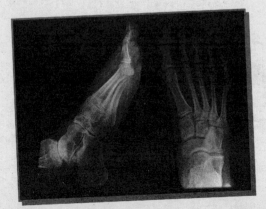

lifetime. That's more than four times around the world!

 The length of your foot is the same as the distance between the inside of your elbow and the inside of your wrist.

Can you "crack" your knuckles? You're not really cracking anything. There's this stuff called synovial fluid in your joints. It contains oxygen, nitrogen, and carbon dioxide; and it lubricates your joints. When you crack a knuckle, you stretch the joint capsule. Gas is released, which forms bubbles, and that's when you hear the crack. In order to crack the same knuckle again, you have to wait until the gases return to the synovial fluid.

Stomach

 Here's a fast fact that will blow your mind. The acid in your stomach is so strong, it will dissolve razor blades!* It's true! Inside your stomach is this stuff called hydrochloric acid that dissolves food and anything else in there.

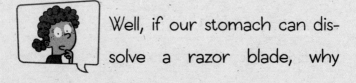 Well, if our stomach can dissolve a razor blade, why

---

* This does *not* mean you should ever eat a razor blade!

doesn't our stomach dissolve *itself*? I'm sure a stomach isn't nearly as strong as a razor blade.

 Good question, Andrea! Your stomach has a protective lining. It's made of mucus covered with sugar molecules that are really good at resisting the acid. Every day, the cells in your stomach get damaged and destroyed. But they're also constantly reproducing themselves. New cells take over for the damaged ones. And believe it or not, your entire stomach lining is replaced about every three days.

That reminds me, our body is always making new skin and getting rid of old skin. Skin cells fall off us all the time. In fact, some of the dust in your house is old dead skin cells. Gross!

 Do you know why your stomach growls?

That's the sound of your digestive juices churning and your stomach muscles getting ready for food. As the juices churn and get moved by your muscles, a lot of 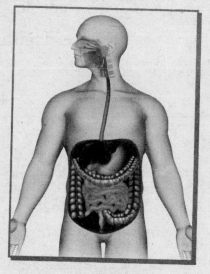 air is squeezed out at either end of your stomach. That's what causes the sound.

Muscles

 You probably think you're pretty strong. After all, you have 639 muscles in your body. But don't be so impressed with yourself. Grasshoppers have about 900 muscles. And you want to hear about an animal that's *really* strong? Caterpillars have *4,000* muscles!

The fastest muscles in your body are in your eyes. They make it possible for you to blink as fast as five times a second. Most days, you blink about fifteen *thousand* times. That's a good thing, because blinking clears away dust particles and lubricates your eyeballs. And by the way, women blink twice as much as men. So we win again!

 I wish you would talk less. You use about a hundred different muscles every time you talk. .

 Arlo, I bet you don't know why we get goose bumps.

Because all the My Weird School books are sold out?

 No! It's because we're mammals. When mammals get cold, the muscles around our hair follicles contract so our hair stands up to make a little extra layer of insulation. We don't have as much hair on our bodies as our ancestors did millions of years ago, but we do still have the little bumps on our skin where the hair would have been. We call those goose bumps.

 Anything else to add about the human body?

Yes! Babies are born without solid kneecaps. It's true! Babies' kneecaps are made out of cartilage, and don't turn into solid bone until the baby is about three years old.

You probably know that everyone has different fingerprints. But we also have different *tongue* prints! So if you ever find yourself at a crime scene, be careful not to lick anything.

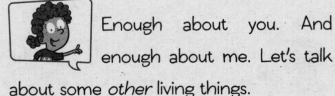 Enough about you. And enough about me. Let's talk about some *other* living things.

Chapter 10

Animals

 You think the human body is weird? Animals are *really* weird. Just the idea of having four legs is weird, if you ask me. A.J. and I dug up some cool fast facts about animals.

 Parrots and rabbits can see behind them, and they don't

even have to turn their heads around. That's because their eyes are on the sides of their heads. So they can watch out for prey that are about to attack them.

The food chain isn't a chain made out of food. That would be weird. A food chain is how energy gets passed from one living thing to another. For example, some grass grows in a field because it has soil, sunlight, and water. A rabbit hops along and eats the grass. A fox runs over, catches the rabbit, and eats it. The fox eventually dies. Bacteria break down its body. It becomes part of the soil. It provides nutrients for new grass. A rabbit eats the grass. And it starts all over again!

 The crowned sandgrouse lives in the Sahara desert in Africa. It may fly as far as thirty miles to find water.

 Some animals don't drink water at *all*. The desert kangaroo rat gets its water only by eating seeds, plants, and insects.

Kangaroo rat

 Then there are camels, of course. Camels are cool. They can drink thirty gallons of water at a time. After that, they can go for days (or even months during the winter) without taking another sip.

 Mayflies are born, live their entire lives, and die as soon as a half hour later. Tortoises, on the other hand, can live 150 years.

Termites eat wood! Can you believe that? So if two ter-mites go to a restaurant, they probably look at the menu and ask the waiter, "What kind of wood do you have?"

 I don't think termites go to restaurants, Arlo.

 Maybe they go to restaurants that are made out of wood.

 Now you're just being silly.

Arlo, do you know why geese fly in a V shape?

 Because if they flew in an X shape they'd be bumping into each other in the middle?

 No! Flying in a V shape conserves their energy. With each bird flying just a little above the bird in front of it, there's less wind resistance. They take turns flying in front so none of them get too tired. Also, flying in a V formation makes it easy to keep track of and communicate with every bird in the group. Jet fighter pilots do the same thing.

An animal needs six things to survive: food, water, shelter, air, a place to raise its young, and video games. Okay, I made up that last one. Animals only need five things to survive.

A.J.'s Top Ten Weirdest Animals

1. Cicadas: Many species spend seventeen years living underground. Then they suddenly come up just to freak everybody out.

2. Andrea!

3. Fleas: They can jump 130 times their own height. Show-offs! If humans could do that, a six-foot

person could jump 780 feet in the air.

4. Dalmatians: As they grow up, most mammals don't change much other than get bigger. But Dalmatian puppies start out all white, and as they get older they develop those black spots.

5. Okapi: They live in Africa and look like giraffes. Their tongues are twelve inches long. They usually use them to get leaves from plants, but they can also clean their own eyes and ears by licking them!

6. Atlantic giant squid: Its eye can be over fifteen inches wide.

7. Hummingbirds: They can't walk, but they're the only bird that can fly backward.

8. Cockroaches: They can live for a few weeks without their head.

9. Starfish: They have no brains. Just like Andrea! Oh, snap! In her face!

10. Flies and butterflies have taste organs on their *feet*! So they can taste anything they land on.

• • • • • • • • • • • • • • •

TRY THIS! You can use crickets to tell the temperature! Male crickets make their chirping noise by rubbing a sharp ridge on one of their wings against the wrinkles, or "files," on their other wing. When it's hot out, they rub their wings faster. So you can tell the temperature by counting how fast a cricket chirps. Just count the number of chirps you hear in fifteen seconds and then add thirty-seven to it. The total will be very close to the outside temperature.

I want one of those cricket thermometers!

"Science is fun. Science is curiosity. We all have natural curiosity. Science is a process of investigating. It's posing questions and coming up with a method."
—Sally Ride

Chapter II

Famous Scientists

 Some kids put up pictures of famous singers or sports heroes on their walls. Not me. In my bedroom I have posters of scientists like Albert Einstein. He was cool. If you ask me, scientists are like rock stars. They should be more famous. Here are some of my favorites. . . .

Marie Curie

Andrea's Top Ten Scientists

1. Galileo Galilei (1564–1642): He was an Italian scientist and scholar who made lots of discoveries in physics and astronomy. Galileo came to be called the Father of Modern Science. He was so good, he was named twice!

WEIRD FACT: The middle finger of Galileo's right hand has been exhibited at the Museo Galileo in Florence, Italy.

2. Isaac Newton (1642–1727): He discovered the law of gravity and the laws of motion. He also developed calculus and built the first reflecting telescope.

WEIRD FACT: He spent one year as a member of the British Parliament, and he only got up to speak once—so he could

tell somebody to close a
window.

3. Gregor Mendel
(1822–1884): He was
an Austrian monk who
founded the science
of genetics. He dis-
covered how heredity
worked by experimenting with peas.

 He did experiments with pee?
Gross! Why would anybody
want to do that?

 Not pee, Arlo! Peas! Mendel
grew more than thirty thou-
sand pea plants in fifteen years.

Doing experiments with peas is pretty weird too, if you ask me.

WEIRD FACT: What Mendel really wanted was to be a high school teacher. But even though he tried teaching a few times, he failed his official teaching exams, twice.

4. Charles Darwin (1809–1882): He was an English naturalist who devised the theory of evolution that says that all species of life evolved from common ancestors.

WEIRD FACT: Darwin and Abraham Lincoln were born on the same day, February 12, 1809.

5. Louis Pasteur (1822–1895): He was a French chemist who is famous for figuring

out what caused disease. He coined the term "vaccine" and created vaccines that saved many lives. When you drink pasteurized milk, it's because of Louis Pasteur.

WEIRD FACT: He was so afraid of catching diseases that he would never shake hands with anyone, not even kings and queens.

6. George Washington Carver (around 1861–1943): He was born a slave and grew up to become a world-famous botanist and inventor. Carver worked a lot with peanuts, sweet potatoes, and soybeans, and figured out how to use them to make face bleach, caramel, chili sauce, glue, ink, metal polish, paper, plastics, rubber,

peanut sausage, shampoo, shaving cream, shoe polish, face powder, and many other products.

WEIRD FACT: Many people think George Washington Carver invented peanut butter, but it had already been around for centuries. But he did help make it popular.

7. Marie Curie (1867–1934): She was a Polish-born French physicist who coined the word "radioactivity" and discovered radium. She was the first woman to win the Nobel Prize, and she won it twice.

WEIRD FACT: What made her famous also killed her. She died

because of exposure to radioactivity. In fact, scientists who want to study her papers have to wear protective clothing so it doesn't happen to them too.

8. Albert Einstein (1879–1955): My hero!* He was a German-born physicist who is famous for his theory of relativity. Hardly anybody understands relativity, but it has something to do with light and speed and time and the universe.**

WEIRD FACT: After he died, Einstein's brain was stolen! The doctor who examined him took his brain and kept it for over forty years. That wasn't very nice.

---

* I think Andrea has a crush on Albert Einstein.

** I do not!

9. Edwin Hubble (1889–1953): He was no relation of Mayor Hubble, who is always in trouble. But the Hubble space telescope was named in his honor. He was an American astronomer whose research helped prove the universe is expanding.

 My underwear keeps expanding. Every so often my mom and I have to go buy some new underwear because the old ones don't fit anymore.

 Quiet, Arlo! This is *my* list.

WEIRD FACT: Edwin Hubble grew up in Missouri, but later he started talking

with an English accent, wearing a cape,
and walking around with a pipe to make
people think he was British.

10. Grace Murray Hopper (1906–
1992): She was an American computer
programmer who did pioneering work on
computer languages. Later she became a
rear admiral in the US Navy.

WEIRD FACT: She is famously associated with the words "bug" and "de-bug." What happened was that she was having a problem with the Navy computer, so she opened up the  computer to find out what was wrong. It turned out there was a moth inside it. It was the first (literal) computer bug.

Bonus: Rachel Carson (1907–1964): She was an American marine biologist who wrote a famous book called *Silent Spring* that played a big part in starting the environmental movement and getting rid of dangerous pesticides like DDT.

WEIRD FACT: As a child, Rachel wanted to be a writer. She had her first story published in a children's magazine when she was only ten years old.

Oops! I like science so much that I chose *eleven* top ten scientists! Sorry!

 Andrea's list of scientists is lame. Here's a list of *my* favorite scientists. . . .

A.J.'s Top Ten Way Cooler Scientists

1. Gideon Sundback: He invented the zipper. If it wasn't for this guy, our pants would be falling down all the time.

WEIRD FACT: Isn't the fact that he

invented the zipper weird enough?

2. Thomas Crapper: He perfected the flush toilet. And his name was Crapper. That's like the washing machine being perfected by a guy named Henry Washingmachine. Notice I put Thomas Crapper second on my list. So he's number two!

3. Dr. Frankenstein: He was a mad scientist who used a secret method to create a monster. That guy was cool.

 Arlo, Frankenstein isn't even a *real* scientist. He's just a fictional character.

 So are you! So nah-nah-nah boo-boo. This is *my* list. Keep quiet.

4. William Herschel: He discovered Uranus.

5. Erasmus Darwin: He was Charles Darwin's brother. He wasn't a scientist, but I feel sorry for him. The Darwin family was probably sitting around the dinner table one night, and the mom said, "Charles created the theory of evolution today. What did you do, Erasmus?" And all Erasmus could say was "Nothin'," or "I picked my nose," or something like that. Poor guy. So I put him on my list.

6. Stubbins Ffirth: He was an American doctor during the 1800s who didn't think that one person could catch yellow fever from another person. To prove it, he covered himself with the vomit, blood,

urine, and saliva from yellow fever patients.

That guy was totally nuts.

7. Nikola Tesla: He was an electrical engineer who got his start working for Thomas Edison and went on to do all kinds of weird research with electricity. He created bolts of artificial lightning and worked on an earthquake machine, a death ray, and an antigravity flying machine. Tesla claimed he had been in contact with aliens from another planet, and he also said he was in love with

a pigeon. Other than that, he was a pretty normal guy. He also has a car named after him.

8. Ben Franklin: You may have heard that he flew a kite in a thunderstorm to experiment with electricity. What you probably don't know is that he tried to electrocute live animals. He even had people over when he tried to electrocute a turkey (and ended up shocking himself instead). His "electric spider" experiment showed how electricity could be used to animate dead creatures. Nothing weird about that, right?

Oh, and he also invented swim fins. Go ahead. Look it up.

9. Bill Richards: I love skateboarding. There are lots of people who say they invented the skateboard, but Bill Richards was the first one to sell them to people. He owned a surf shop in California called Val Surf with his teenage son Mark. In 1962, after he saw some kids riding surfboards to which they'd attached wheels, he ordered some roller skate wheels himself and began selling "sidewalk surfboards" so his customers could surf anytime. And the rest is history!

10. My great-uncle Ernie: He discovered the law of towels.

Chapter 12

Fakes, Frauds, and Fame

I think you kids should be aware that all science isn't *real* science. All scientists aren't real scientists. For money, fame, or other reasons, fake scientists have created weird curiosities and pretended they were rare scientific discoveries. Weirdly, a lot of them were British. Here are a few science hoaxes. . . .

- The Bunny Babies

In 1726, a British woman named Mary Toft gave birth to nine baby rabbits. Or that was what she claimed anyway. She became famous, of course, and later she had other litters of rabbit babies. But when a servant was caught trying to sneak a rabbit into Toft's room, the hoax was exposed.

- The Fiji Mermaid

In 1842, an Englishman named Dr. J. Griffin came to New York with the body of a mermaid that he said had been caught in the Pacific Ocean. Thousands came to his lectures, where Griffin claimed the ocean was filled with sea-people, the same way we have lions on land and sea lions in the water. A lot of people fell for it, until it was discovered that "Dr. Griffin" was actually a business partner of the circus showman P. T. Barnum, and the "mermaid" was just the upper body of an ape that had been sewn to the body of a fish.

• The Cardiff Giant

In 1869, workers digging a well in New York State discovered the petrified body of a ten-foot-tall man. It was a huge sensation. Actually, a guy named George Hull created the giant as a prank. P. T. Barnum offered him sixty thousand dollars just to rent it for three months and put it on display. Hull said no, so Barnum made his own fake version of the original fake and put *that* on display. Hull sued Barnum, but a judge threw the case out because Hull couldn't prove the Cardiff Giant was real, and there's nothing wrong with making a fake version of a fake original.

• Piltdown Man

In 1912, a weird set of bone fragments, including a human skull and an ape's jawbone, was discovered in England. Many British scientists believed the bones were from an ancient creature that was the missing link between apes and humans. It wasn't until 1953 that it was revealed that Piltdown Man was a fake. Somebody had taken a modern human skull and combined it with an ape's jawbone with the teeth filed down.

The Piltdown Man was shown to be a hoax in 1953.

- Crop Circles

This one was more recent, and it also took place in England. In the 1970s, a bunch of huge, perfectly formed circles started appearing mysteriously in wheat fields. Even respected scientists had no explanation for them. Could they have been the work of aliens from outer space? Mystical energy fields? Secret messages from dead people?

Finally, in 1991, a couple of pranksters named Doug Bower and Dave Chorley admitted that they used some planks, rope, and wire to create the crop circles.

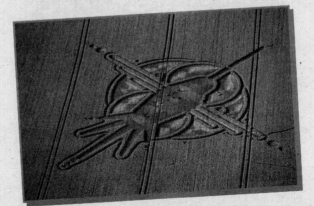

Really Bad
Science Jokes

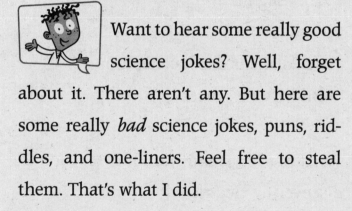

Want to hear some really good science jokes? Well, forget about it. There aren't any. But here are some really *bad* science jokes, puns, riddles, and one-liners. Feel free to steal them. That's what I did.

Why can't you believe anything atoms say?

Because they make up everything.

How do you cut the ocean in half?

With a sea saw.

How do trees get online?

They log in.

How do aliens drink coffee?

On a flying saucer.

What was Benjamin Franklin's reaction to discovering electricity?

He was shocked.

What do you do with a dead chemist?

Barium.

Why did the dinosaur cross the road?

Because there were no chickens in those days.

I hear there's a new restaurant on the moon.

The food is good, but there's no atmosphere.

A neutron walked into a bar and asked how much a drink would cost.

The bartender said, "For you, no charge."

What runs faster, cold or hot?

Hot. Because you can catch a cold.

People who run around in circles all the time are crazy.

Planets that do the same thing are orbiting.

Why did the scientist remove the doorbell from his house?

He wanted to win the Nobel Prize.

Two blood cells fell in love.

Sadly, it was all in vein.

How do we know Saturn was married before?

It has a lot of rings.

What did the earth say to Mars?

Get a life.

Two tectonic plates bumped into each other.

One of them said, "Sorry, it was my fault."

A mushroom walks into a bar, but the bartender won't serve him.

"Why not?" asks the mushroom. "I'm a fungi."

Two atoms were talking, and one of them said, "I think I lost a proton."

The other said, "Oh no! Are you sure?"

"Yes, I'm positive."

Why can't you hear a pterodactyl going to the bathroom?

Because the "*p*" is silent.

What do you call two dinosaurs that crash into each other?

Tyrannosaurus wrecks.

Did you hear about the chemistry teacher

who threw sodium chloride at his students?

He was arrested for a salt.

 Wow, those were really awful, Arlo! Well, it looks like we're coming to the end of the book now. How do I know? Because there are hardly any pages left. Just to be sure, I counted them. That's science!

 Not so fast! We still have to talk about my favorite subject.

The Science of Grossness

 Well, it's about time! Finally, I get to write this whole chapter by myself. Andrea and her snooty friends don't like it when I talk about pooping and peeing and farting. She thinks it's disgusting. But show me a kid who claims they don't poop, pee, or fart, and I'll show you a liar.

So let's get started! It might be a good idea to not eat anything while you read this chapter.*

The Science of Farts

When you eat, the food gets broken down in your intestines by bacteria. Some of it is made into hydrogen sulfide gas. And that stuff smells like rotten eggs. P.U.! Foods that have a lot of sulfur, like beans or cabbage, make it worse. So does broccoli, Brussels sprouts, and soda. Most people cut the cheese at least ten times a day. That's a half a quart of gas! Hey, we should find a way to use that gas to power

---

* I would just like to say for the record that I am participating in this book under protest.

cars and stuff. That would be cool. You could call them "fart cars."

Farting is nothing to be ashamed of. It's completely natural, and everybody does it. Your parents fart, even if they don't admit it. Your teacher farts. The pope farts. Even Andrea farts.

 Are you finished, Arlo? This is disgusting.

 Almost. I'd just like to add that your farts smell worse than mine.

 What? That's not true!

It is too. Females have more concentrated hydrogen sulfide in their bodies than males, so their farts smell worse. Go look it up if you don't believe me.

 You're impossible!

The Science of Snot

 Every time you take a breath of air through your nose, other stuff gets in there too: germs, dust, soot, bacteria. Yuck. Remember those little hairs inside your nose? They stop some of this stuff. But they can't stop it all.

Luckily, we have this thing that lines the external cavities of the body called the mucous membrane. That would be a good name for a rock band, by the way. The Mucous Membrains.

Anyway, the mucous membrane is constantly producing slimy stuff called mucus, of course. It catches stuff like flypaper, and the next thing you know, it's time to do some major nose mining. Snot is just a form of mucus, which lubricates and protects your body.

I'm really sorry to tell you this, but every day you swallow about a quart of mucus. You're welcome! Isn't the human body wonderful?

The Science of Burping

If you don't want to say "burping," you can say "eructation." That's what scientists call it.

Let's say you eat a piece of pizza ("You eat a piece of pizza!"). The bread, cheese, sauce, and toppings go down your throat and into your stomach. But something else makes its way down there too. Air!

Air contains gases like nitrogen and oxygen. There's nothing wrong with that.

The only problem is, there isn't a whole lot of room in your stomach. Your body doesn't need the gases, so it gets rid of them. That's where burping comes in. The stomach squeezes itself, and the air is forced up and out of your esophagus, which is a tube that connects the back of the throat to your stomach. *Burp!*

By the way, gorillas make a burping sound when they want to let other gorillas know they're not threatening.

I can burp the whole alphabet, which is cool. If you want to make some really good burps, drink some soda first. It contains a gas called carbon dioxide that will really get you burping.

But if you think burping is gross and disgusting, there are a few things you can do that will help you cut down on your burping. Stop using straws (air gets inside them). Eat slower. Don't talk with your mouth full of food.

And if those things don't work, here's a tip—just turn some music up really loud so people can't hear you burp.

The Science of Sweating

Sweat is gross. But we have to do it because that's how our body cools itself off. It's like a natural air conditioner.

Do you know what the sweatiest parts of your body are? Your feet! It's true. They have 250,000 sweat glands in them, and they produce about a cup of sweat a day. Yuck.

Here's a good question to ask your parents. Why do people in really hot countries have such spicy food? The answer is that spicy food increases the activity of your sweat glands, and that cools down the body.

The Science of Bad Breath

When you wake up in the morning, do you have this horrible taste in your mouth? Yuck! Me too. I could brush my teeth for a million hundred hours before I go to sleep, but I'm still going to wake up with my mouth tasting like an old sneaker. Bad breath is so yucky that scientists don't even call it that. They call it "halitosis."

Why do we have it? The inside of your mouth is wet all the time, night and day. You're constantly producing saliva, or spit. Mostly, saliva is made of water. But while you're sleeping, your mouth doesn't make as much saliva. Bacteria build up in there. Millions of them. That's why you wake up with halitosis.

The Science of Earwax

How come scientists are always making up new words for stuff? Do you know what they call earwax? They call it "cerumen." Earwax is made from sweat, oil, dirt, and dead skin. It protects the ear from substances like dirt and even insects. What? I have bugs in my ears? Help! Somebody call an ambulance!

Our nurse at school, Mrs. Cooney, told us that we should never put anything into our ear except our elbow. That makes no sense at all because you can't reach your ear with your elbow. And believe me, I tried. So I found a solution to that problem. I put my elbow in my friend Ryan's ear.

The Science of Pee
You probably know what scientists call pee. They call it "urine." Sometimes my dad sings an old song called "Urine the Money." That's weird. I don't know what

pee has to do with money.

Pee is cool. Think about it: You drink a chocolate milk shake and it comes out yellow. You drink some purple grape juice and it comes out yellow. In fact, you drink anything that's *any* color and it comes out yellow. What's up with *that*?

What happens is that when you eat or drink, your body can only use some of that stuff for energy. The rest is waste and we have to get rid of it. Our kidneys are these four-inch organs that sit in our upper abdominal area. They're shaped like kidney beans, so they have the perfect name. We have two of them, but one is enough to get the job done.

While you're playing ball or walking

your dog, the blood in your body is getting pumped through your kidneys. Basically, they wash it, filtering out things your body can't use. What's left is pee. Your kidneys wash forty-four gallons of blood every day. They also balance fluids by getting rid of extra water. The stuff that makes pee yellow is a pigment called "urochrome."

The average person will produce up to two quarts of urine a day. Almost all of it is water. The rest is wastes, salts, and ammonia. I guess that's the stuff that makes it smell. So when you pee, aim carefully!

The Science of Poop

I saved the worst for last. Poop!

Oh no. Here we go.

 Poop is part of life, Andrea. It's also gross. You can blame it all on eating. If we could figure out a way to stop eating, we'd figure out a way to stop pooping.

As soon as you put a piece of food in your mouth, your body starts to attack it (by chewing!). Some of that food will be useful to build strong bones and muscles. Some of it won't. Your body wants to get rid of the useless stuff.

Just seven seconds after you take a bite of something, that food is in your stomach.

Over the next four hours, your stomach attacks it with acids to break it down.

That food is already yucky, but it's not poop yet. It needs to be pushed out of your stomach and into your small intestine. I don't know why they call it a *small* intestine, because it isn't small at all. It's over twenty feet long! Lucky for you your small intestine is curled up inside your body. It would be weird if it wasn't.

Anyway, the small intestine is covered with these little things called villi. They look like tiny fingers. The villi go through all the yucky stuff that comes down the pipe and sorts it into fats, proteins, and carbohydrates.

What's left after that goes into the large

intestine. I don't know why they call it a large intestine, because it isn't large at all. It's only about five feet long, but it's much wider. Part of the large intestine is called the colon. It's not like the colon on your computer keyboard. Completely different. If you had one of those colons on your keyboard, you'd want to clean it off right away. You might even want to get a new keyboard. Anyway, the colon absorbs any last water and minerals, and what's left after that is . . . ta da! Poop!

 Are you finished talking about poop, Arlo?

 Almost. The average adult

produces about just under a pound of poop every day. You know what that means. It must be somebody's job to weigh poop! Yuck! I feel sorry for that guy. That's why you should go to college. If you don't, you might become a professional poop weigher.

The Ending

Are you finished talking about poop *now*, Arlo?

Yes, but since you asked, here's one last fast fact for you. A dung beetle eats poop! It's also the world's strongest animal. It can pull more than a thousand times its own body weight. That's like a person pulling six double-decker buses. And we don't spend the whole day eating poop!

 Okay! Well, I can see you two have learned a lot about science!

 I still have more questions, Mr. Docker.

That's great! I love questions! That's why I became a science teacher in the first place. Fire away!

How can we believe anything atoms say if they make up everything?

Huh? What?

If there's a new moon every month, where does the old one go?

I . . . uh . . .

How can fish hold their breath for so long underwater?

They don't. . . .

If corn oil is made from corn and olive oil is made from olives, where does baby oil come from?

Wait. What?

If you cry underwater, how does anybody know?

I never thought about it.

If bread is square, why is sand-wich meat round?

 Oh, dear, I'm sorry. Look at the time. I have a meeting to get to.

 How come grown-ups always have meetings to get to when-ever I ask them questions?

 Don't go, Mr. Docker! I have more science questions to ask too. We haven't even scratched the sur-face yet.

 Why would you want to

scratch a surface? That could damage the surface. My mom told me that if I scratch the surface of the table in the dining room, I'm in big trouble. That's why we use place mats.

 I guess there's just too much science to fit in this book. If you can learn about the science of poop, you could learn about the science of *anything*. You could learn about the science of rocket ships. The science of dinosaurs. The science of fireworks . . .

 Hey, I just googled "the science of fireworks." Did you know that there are no true blue fireworks? They still haven't found the right combination of chemicals to make a deep, bright blue when it explodes. I didn't know that!

 Me neither. Maybe we should have included a Chapter 15.

 Science is really interesting.

 See what I mean? You should poke around, Arlo. Ask your parents to help you go online and search for stuff. You can also go to your local library and look for other books on subjects that interest you.

Ugh, Andrea said the B word! Yuck! Disgusting! I think I'm gonna throw up!

 Oh, stop it, Arlo. I know you love learning new things.

 Maybe we'll find out what color pumpkins are. Maybe I'll go windsurfing on Neptune. Maybe atoms will sit still and stop making everything up. Maybe Andrea will fix her broken hair. Maybe we'll use a lever to pick up the earth. Maybe I'll cook a hundred thousand pieces of toast. Maybe racing cars will drive upside down on the ceiling. Maybe I'll get those drums removed from my ears. Maybe we'll find out where baby oil comes from. Maybe they'll open up some new restaurants for termites. Maybe okapi will stop licking their own eyeballs. Maybe Henry Washingmachine will get credit for his invention. Maybe a dung beetle will pull a double-decker bus.

But it won't be easy!

Afterword

The Secret of the Universe

 Okay, are you ready to hear the secret of the universe?

Are you on pins and needles?

Well, you should really sit on a chair. It hurts to be on pins and needles.

Okay, here goes . . .

The secret to the universe . . . isn't here!

What, did you *really* think I was going

to tell you the secret of the universe? I'm an eight-year-old kid! I barely even know how to tie my shoes.

I've got news for you. *Nobody* knows the secret of the universe. Not even the smartest scientists! So go back to page 1 and read the book from start to finish. You just might learn something.*

"Imagination is more important than knowledge. Knowledge is limited. Imagination encircles the world."
—Albert Einstein

---

* Nah-nah-nah boo-boo on you!

"I'm sure the universe is full of
intelligent life. It's just been too
intelligent to come here."
—Arthur C. Clarke

"Basic research is what I am doing when
I don't know what I'm doing."
—Wernher von Braun

"If we knew what it was we were
doing, it would not be called
research, would it?"
—Albert Einstein

"The good thing about science
is that it's true whether or not you
believe in it."
—Neil deGrasse Tyson

"My goal is simple. It is complete understanding of the universe, why it is as it is and why it exists at all."
—Stephen Hawking

"Living on Earth may be expensive, but it includes an annual free trip around the Sun."
—Seen on a bumper sticker

"The science of today is the technology of tomorrow."
—Edward Teller

"The best way to have a good idea is to have a lot of ideas."
—Linus Pauling

"Science never solves a problem
without creating ten more."
—George Bernard Shaw

"Science knows no country, because
knowledge belongs to humanity, and is
the torch which illuminates the world."
—Louis Pasteur

"It is better to know some of the
questions than all of the answers."
—James Thurber

"It is the same with people as it is with
riding a bike. Only when moving can one
comfortably maintain one's balance."
—Albert Einstein